ONE JUMP RING
endless possibilities for **chain mail** jewelry

Lauren Andersen

KALMBACH BOOKS

Waukesha, Wisconsin

Kalmbach Books
21027 Crossroads Circle
Waukesha, Wisconsin 53186
www.JewelryAndBeadingStore.com

Published in 2017
21 20 19 18 17   1 2 3 4 5

Manufactured in China

ISBN: 978-1-62700-303-2
EISBN: 978-1-62700-304-9

Editor: Erica Swanson
Book Design: Lisa Schroeder
Photographer: William Zuback

Library of Congress Control Number: 2016943718

CONTENTS

INTRODUCTION

Welcome to the world of chain mail! This book uses only one size jump ring to complete all the projects in the book: 18-gauge 3/16" (or 4.75mm). I have also made all of the bracelets size 7" and adjustable to a size 7½", with the exception of the "Beaded Four Leaf Clover Bracelet," "Double Flower Bracelet," and "Angel Wings Bracelet." If you need your bracelet to be longer than 7½", you can always extend the chain attached to the end of each bracelet.

I chose to use enamel-coated copper jump rings because I feel they are the easiest to manipulate. You will not have to use brute strength to open and close your jump rings. And they come in such brilliant colors!

Each project will have an introduction, a list of materials needed for the project, and the tools needed to complete the piece. Some of the projects also include tips that you may find helpful.

I will tell you how to set up your basic workspace, how to open and close jump rings so they are flush, and the importance of the orientation of clasps and earring wires. I will also teach you how to make your own earring wires and clasps and how to make double-loop bead connectors. It is not necessary to learn how to make your own components, but it will help you extend your jewelry-making techniques.

Chain mail jump rings are more commonly measured by their inside diameter. Each seller of chain mail jump rings uses either inches or millimeters to measure the inside diameter of their jump rings. You will be using an 18-gauge 3/16" jump ring or an 18-gauge 4.75mm jump ring. They are interchangeable.

I have used enamel-coated jump rings in my projects, but you can use sterling silver, silver-filled, copper, brass, or any other metal as well. You may find that the anodized aluminum jump rings are a bit larger. I hope you enjoy your journey into the world of chain mail!

— Lauren, The ChainMaille Lady™

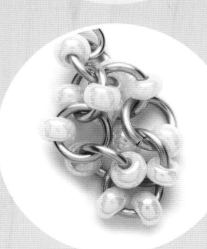

BASICS

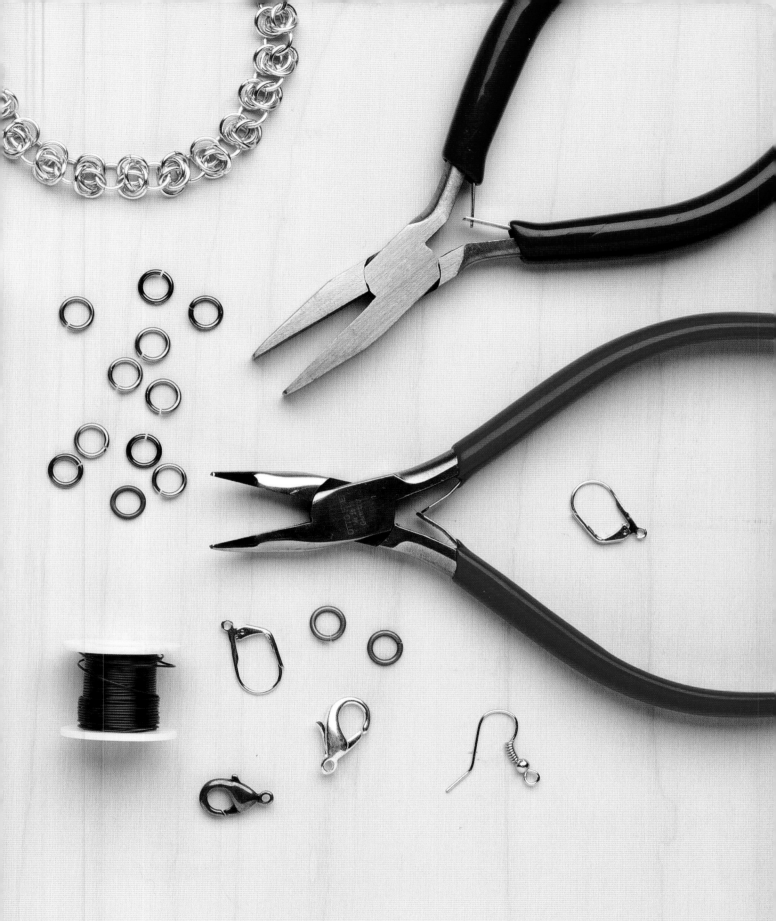

Setting Up Your Workspace

To make chain mail, you will need two pairs of comfortable, non-serrated pliers with double leaf-springs, a bead mat. And you will also need jump rings, of course!

JUMP RINGS

A jump ring is a circle of wire that can be opened and connected to other jump rings in various combinations to make chain mail. This book is all about using only one size (measured from inner diameter) and gauge (thickness) of jump ring: 18-gauge 3/16" (4.75mm). I like to use enamel-coated copper jump rings, as they are affordable and easy to work with. You could also substitute other metals, such as sterling silver, copper, bronze, aluminum, and even stainless steel (although these will be hard to open and close, so I do not recommend them for beginners). Choose the color you like, or follow my examples.

PLIERS

Your biggest challenge may be choosing what type of pliers to use and in what combination. Some people mix and match chainnose pliers with bent-nose pliers or snubnose pliers with flatnose pliers. Pliers can range in price from $5 to more than $80. I've listed the different types of pliers and what they are generally used for.

1. Chainnose pliers: These are the most common type of pliers used in chain mail. They taper to a point, and the inside of the jaws are smooth, not serrated. The jaw length varies from 20–25mm.

2. Snubnose pliers: These are becoming more common in chain mail. They also taper to a point; however, the jaw length is much shorter than a standard pair of chain mail pliers. The jaw length is 14mm. Overall length is 5¼".

3. Flatnose pliers: Like the name implies, instead of having a pointed end, they are flat across the end.

4. Bentnose pliers: These are like chainnose pliers with a bend in them. Some people use the bend to open and close their jump rings and the pointed tip when needed to get into small places.

Nylon-jaw pliers: These pliers are helpful for straightening wire without marring it.

Bail-making pliers: The barrels of these pliers aren't tapered. This tool is a helpful dowel for turning earring wires and clasps.

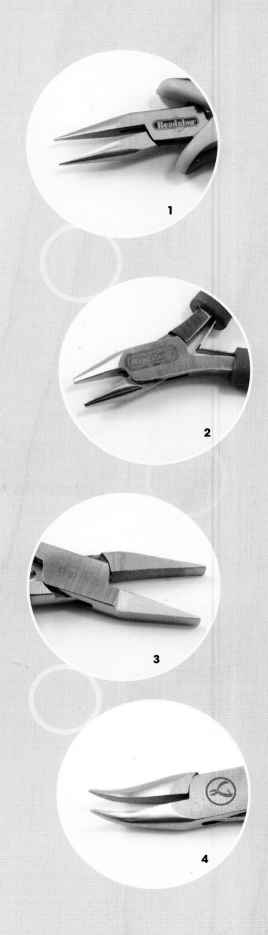

1

2

3

4

OTHER ITEMS

5. Bead mats: A work surface keeps all of your jump rings from scattering everywhere. Bead mats are made from a non-linty material and come in a variety of colors.

6. Task lamp: These lamps come in all shapes and sizes. Lighting is very important. Lamps brighten your workspace considerably and make it easier to view your project.

7 and **8. Magnification:** Seeing the jump rings and ensuring that they are closed properly is very important. Magnification will help you to accomplish this. A task lamp and magnification are not necessary, but they are extremely helpful for making nicely finished jewelry.

5

6

7

8

Basic Techniques

Chain mail is easy to start, because you only need to learn a few techniques before beginning!

OPENING AND CLOSING JUMP RINGS

This is the most important technique to master in chain mail. It takes patience and practice. When you first see your jump rings, they may look like they are already open—but they are not. You will need to open them further and close them tighter in order to weave them into patterns. It is a good idea to practice closing jump rings because eventually, every jump ring will need to be closed. Try to keep your pliers in your hands at all times while you are weaving. This will help you to keep your place in the weave.

Plier Placement

1. Place the pliers in your hands with your thumb and index finger as close to the jaw of the pliers as is comfortable. This will give you better control and leverage over your pliers and your work.

2. If you grip the pliers too far back on the handles, you will not have the leverage you need to close heavier gauge jump rings.

3. If you grip the jump ring too vertically, it will cause unnecessary stress on your joints and it will also make it difficult to maneuver the jump ring.

4. If you grip the jump ring too horizontally, you will not have enough leverage. This also puts stress on your neck and shoulders.

Closing a Jump Ring

5. Place the split in the jump ring at the 12 o'clock position and place the tips of the pliers as close to the split in the jump ring as possible. Notice how close my hands are to the tips of the pliers?

6. Bring your dominant hand forward and your non-dominant hand away from you; at the same time, press the ends of the jump ring inward towards each other. The inward pressure is critical. Without it, you will never get the jump ring completely closed. The ends of the jump ring will overlap slightly.

7. Now, reverse the motion performed in step 6: Bring your non-dominant hand forward and your dominant hand back, and again press the ends of the jump ring inwards towards each other. Notice how the ends again overlap.

8. Now, bring your dominant hand forward, evening out the ends of the jump ring. Wiggle the ends into position by pushing and pulling the ends in tiny motions, so you get a seamless closure.

Opening a Jump Ring

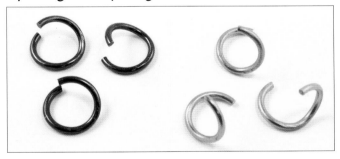

9. To open a jump ring, repeat step 6. You will open the jump ring wide enough to be able to scoop up or weave through other jump ring. The purple jump rings on the left are an example of properly open jump rings. The gold jump rings on the right are open too wide and will be difficult to close properly while keeping the jump ring round at the same time.

MAKING A CLASP

Make your own clasp to coordinate perfectly with the color and style of your handmade chain mail jewelry. This technique is easy to master and so very affordable!

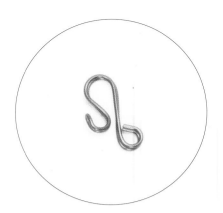

materials

» 20-gauge craft or silver wire, approximately 4½" long

tools

» ruler
» bail-making pliers (small barrels: 4mm and 2mm)
» nylon-jaw pliers (optional)
» wire cutters

1. Cut a 4½"-long piece of 20-gauge wire.

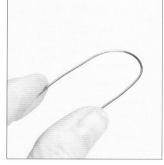

2. Place the tips of the wire together and work your way up the wire to the top. Using your fingers, fold the wire in half, making sure that the wires stay parallel to one another.

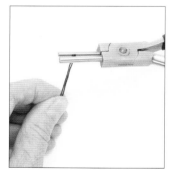

3. Use nylon-jaw pliers to get the bend at the top as close together as possible. Use little squeezes with the pliers to close. There will be a small space between the closure—that is perfectly OK.

4. Use the small bail-making pliers (the 4mm barrel should be facing you and the 2mm barrel should be facing away from you). Place the folded portion of the wire in between the jaws of the pliers, making sure the folded part of the wire is even with the barrels.

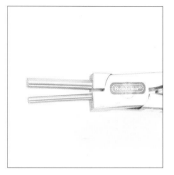
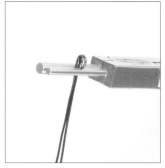

5. With your thumb, press the wire around the small 2mm barrel about three quarters of the way around the 2mm barrel. Release the wire from the jaws of the pliers. The bend in the wire will look like a hook.

6. Flip the pliers over so now the 2mm barrel is facing you and the 4mm barrel is facing away from you.

7. Place the wire between the jaws of the pliers with the hook portion of the wire facing you.

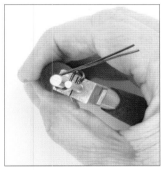

8. With your thumb, press the wire around the larger 4mm barrel until the touches the hook. Release the wire from the pliers.

9. If the ends of your wire are not equal, use the flat edge of the wire cutters to even them up.

10. With the 4mm barrel facing you, insert the wire between the jaws with the bent portion of the clasp toward you and parallel to the barrels.

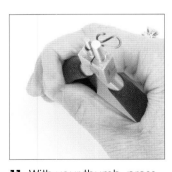

11. With your thumb, press the wire around the small 2mm barrel until the wire touches the cut ends and forms a closed circle. Release the wire from the jaws of the pliers.

MAKING EARRING WIRES

With this technique, you can match your earring wires to the jump rings in your project. You can purchase pre-made earring wires, but it is not always easy to get that perfect color—so I will show you how to make an earring wire using bail-making pliers and roundnose pliers.

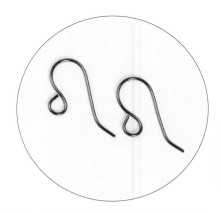

Materials
» **2** pieces of 18-gauge or 20-gauge craft or silver wire, each 2" long

Tools
» ruler
» bail-making pliers (large barrels: 8mm and 5mm)
» nylon-jaw pliers, for straightening the wire as necessary
» chainnose or flatnose pliers
» roundnose pliers
» nylon hammer (optional)
» cup burr, nail file, or small file

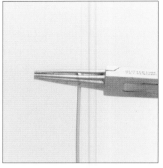

1. Cut two pieces of either 18-gauge or 20-gauge wire 2" long. (The green wire is 20-gauge and the yellow wire is 18-gauge.)

2. Using roundnose pliers, determine how large of a loop you need for the earring. Mark your pliers with a permanent marker so the loops will match on both of the earrings.

3. Place the wire between the jaws of the roundnose pliers at the mark that you made in step 2. Make sure the top of the wire is flush with the pliers.

TIP **If you prefer to purchase earring wires, a good rule of thumb is to buy pre-made silver-plated wires for light colored jump rings and gold-plated wires for the darker colored jump rings.**

4. With your thumb, push the wire away from you around the jaw of the pliers all the way around until the wire touches the cut end on top, forming a closed loop.

5. Hold the bail-making pliers so the small 5mm barrel is close to you and the large 8mm barrel is farther away from you.

6. Place the wire between the jaws of the bail-making pliers with the "P" up above the jaws and facing you.

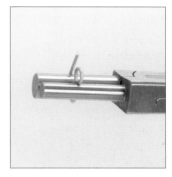

7. With your thumb, push the wire away from you and around the large barrel of the plier all the way around until it almost touches the loop.

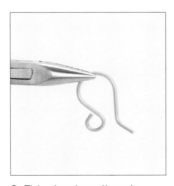

8. This step is optional: Make a slight ⅛" bend at the end of the earring wire using either chainnose or flatnose pliers.

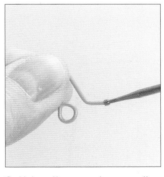

9. Using the cup burr, nail file, or small file, file the end of the earring wire to remove any sharp edges. (The cup bur rounds the ends of the wire.) Place the end of the wire into the cup, push the two firmly together, and twist the tool against the wire for a smooth, round end.

10. Use the a nylon-jaw hammer to work-harden the finished earring wire: Place the ear wire on a hard surface (like a bench block) and lightly hit the wire with the hammer.

MAKING DOUBLE-LOOP BEAD CONNECTORS

This technique offers a way to add beads to your work. It will make the ends of the wire look like a double jump ring. You can choose wire that matches the color of the jump rings. This example showcases a 6mm bead, but you can add larger or smaller beads, crystals, and pearls, if desired. When using different size beads, you'll need to adjust the wire length. (Use a longer piece of wire if you're unsure. It's better to have too much wire than not enough!)

materials

» 18-gauge wire approximately 4" long per bead for the beads used in this book

tools

» ruler
» bail-making pliers, small (barrels: 4mm and 2mm)
» nylon-jaw pliers for straightening the wire as necessary
» wire cutters

1. Cut one piece of 18-gauge wire approximately 4" long.

2. Hold the bail-making pliers parallel with the small barrel (2mm) facing you and the large barrel (4mm) facing away from you.

3. Grip one end of the wire between the pliers with the top of the wire flush with the top of the pliers.

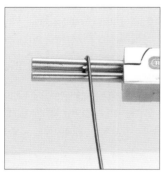

4. Holding the pliers in your dominant hand, place your other hand below the pliers and on the wire. Slowly bend the wire upward and around the 4mm jaw of the plier until the wire touches the point in between the pliers and slightly to the right of the end of the wire.

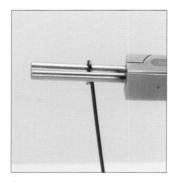

5. Relax the pliers and rotate the wire until the tail is below the plier's jaw, like it was in step 3.

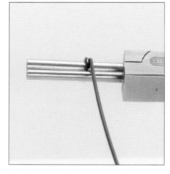

6. Re-grip the wire with the pliers, and with your non-dominant hand, bend the wire upward and to the right of the previous wrap. Bend the wire until it crosses the point in between the pliers.

7. Relax the pliers and rotate the wire until the tail is below the plier's jaw, like it was in step 3.

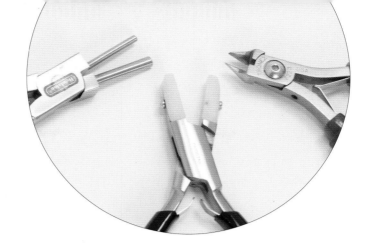

8. Repeat steps 6 and 7 until you have two and half loops on the wire.

9. Remove the loops from the wire and use wire cutters to trim the wire to two loops.

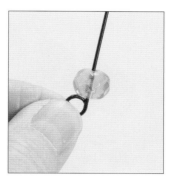

10. String a bead on the uncoiled end of the wire.

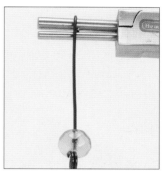

11. With the rings that you made facing you, repeat steps 2–5, but wrapping the wire in the opposite direction from the first loop.

12. Repeat step 6, wrapping the loops in the opposite direction from the first set of loops, until the loops are snug against the bead.

13. Remove the loops from the wire and trim the wire. You may have an extra loop; trim that off as well.

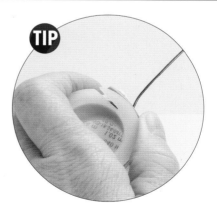

TIP

I leave the wire on the spool and extend it from the spool, straightening the wire by pressing it between nylon-jaw pliers before cutting it. That allows me to use the spool for leverage while I'm straightening the wire.

PROJECTS

Vessel
Necklace

I fell in love with this vessel
when I first laid eyes on it,
and I knew I had to make a
necklace showcasing my
treasure. Not finding a chain
that I liked that would do this
vessel justice, I decided to make
my own! This is a very, very
simple necklace to make. Feel
free to use the perfect color that
will complement your vessel
or charm. I made mine long
enough to go over my head,
so no clasp needed!

» PREPARE: Close 2 jump rings. Open all the remaining jump rings.

Make the Necklace

materials

» **156** jump rings (gunmetal enamel-coated copper)
» **1** vessel or charm

tools

» **2** pairs chainnose, snubnose, flatnose, or bentnose pliers

1. Take one open jump ring and scoop up two closed jump rings. Close the jump ring.

2. Take one open jump ring and scoop up the same two closed jump rings added in step 1. Close the jump ring.

3. Take one open jump ring and scoop up the two closed jump rings added in step 1. Close the jump ring.

4. Take one open jump ring and scoop up the same two closed jump rings that you picked up in step 3. Close the jump ring.

5. Take one open jump ring and scoop up the two jump rings added in steps 3 and 4. Close the jump ring.

6. Take a second open jump ring and repeat step 5.

7. Repeat steps 5 and 6, picking up the last two jump rings added, for the length of the necklace.

8. Before you connect the ends of the necklace together with two open jump rings, slip on your vessel or charm. If, like my vessel, it is too small to slip onto the chain, connect the two ends together and then add the vessel to any of the two jump rings in the chain.

Three-by-One Bracelet

This is a simple yet elegant piece. I made mine using gold-colored rings and they look just like the real thing! It would also make a lovely charm bracelet—all you would have to do is to add charms to the single jump rings.

» PREPARE: Close 57 jump rings. Open 26 jump rings.

Make the Bracelet

materials

» **83** jump rings (gold enamel-coated copper)
» **1** gold-plated clasp
» **1** gold-plated charm (optional)

tools

» **2** pairs chainnose, snubnose, flatnose, or bentnose pliers

1. Take one open jump ring and scoop up three closed jump rings. Before closing the jump ring, add the clasp. Close the jump ring.

2. Take one open jump ring and scoop up three closed jump rings, then scoop up the three closed jump rings added in step 1. Close the jump ring.

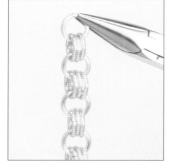

3. Continue scooping up three jump rings and attaching them to the three previous closed jump rings with one open jump ring. Make the bracelet as long as you need. End by scooping up the last three closed jump rings on the chain and not adding three new closed jump rings. Close the jump ring.

4. I added a length of 1+1 chain to the end of my bracelet to make the size adjustable. Take one open jump ring and scoop up the last single jump ring added in step 3. Close the jump ring.

5. I added a total of six jump rings to the end of my bracelet. On the sixth jump ring, I added a bumblebee charm. Feel free to add any charm you like.

3-4-5-4-3 Earrings

These earrings are so simple, you can make a pair in about 15 minutes! The main version is a patriotic pair in red, white, and blue. For an alternate color combination (see p. 27), I chose the traditional colors of Mardi Gras. Rex, the King of Carnival, selected this scheme in 1892, declaring purple for justice, green for faith, and gold for power.

» PREPARE: Open and close all of the jump rings for one pair of earrings at a time. Lay them out in columns:

First column: 2 closed red jump rings and 1 open red jump ring

Second column: 2 closed egg white jump rings and 2 open egg white jump rings

Third column: 3 closed silver blue jump rings and 2 open silver blue jump rings

Fourth column: 2 closed egg white jump rings and 2 open egg white jump rings

Fifth column: 2 closed red jump rings and 1 open red jump ring

Make the Earrings

materials

- » **12** jump rings (red enamel-coated copper)
- » **16** jump rings (egg white enamel-coated copper)
- » **12** jump rings (silver blue enamel-coated copper)
- » **1** pair earring wires (see "Making Earring Wires," p. 14)

tools

- » **2** pairs chainnose, snubnose, flatnose, or bentnose pliers

1. Beginning with the first column, take one open red jump ring and scoop up two closed red jump rings. Close the jump ring. Lay it back in the first column.

2. From the second column, take one open egg white jump ring and scoop up two closed egg white jump rings. Close the jump ring.

3. From the second column, take one open egg white jump ring and scoop up one of the closed egg white jump rings added in step 2. Close the jump ring. Lay it back in the second column.

4. From the third column, take one open silver blue jump ring and scoop up two closed silver blue jump rings. Close the jump ring.

5. From the third column, take one open silver blue jump ring and scoop up one of the closed silver blue jump ring added in step 4. Before closing, add one closed silver blue jump ring. Close the jump ring. Lay it back in the third column.

6. From the fourth column, take one open egg white jump ring and scoop two closed egg white jump rings. Close the jump ring.

7. From the fourth column, take one open egg white jump ring and scoop up one of the closed egg white jump rings added in step 6. Close the jump ring. Lay it back in the fourth column.

8. From the fifth column, take one open red jump ring and scoop up two closed red jump rings to it. Close the jump ring. Lay it back in the fifth column.

9. Take one open silver blue jump ring and add the red chain from column one, the egg white chain from column two, the silver blue chain from column three, the egg white chain from column four, the red chain from column five, and finally the earring wire. Close the jump ring.

10. Repeat to make a second earring.

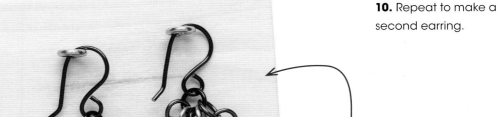

Color Option

Scale Earrings

Since scales are available in many different sizes
and colors, you can make a pair of scale mail earrings
to match each outfit! Anodized aluminum scales are very
lightweight and colorful—perfect for large earrings
that don't stretch or pull.

» PREPARE: Open all 30 jump rings.

Make the Earrings

materials

» **30** jump rings (pink enamel-coated copper)
» **20** small scales, 14.3x22.2mm (⁹⁄₁₆x⁷⁄₈") (pink anodized aluminum)
» **1** pair earring wires (see "Making Earring Wires," p. 14)

tools

» **2** pairs chainnose, snubnose, flatnose, or bentnose pliers

1. Take one open jump ring scoop up one scale. Close the jump ring. Repeat to add a jump ring to each scale.

2. Take one open jump ring and add an earring wire and two jump rings with scales. Close the jump ring.

3. Take one open jump ring and scoop up the jump ring added in step 2. Make sure that you have one jump ring with a scale to the left of the new open jump ring and one jump ring with a scale to the right of the new open jump ring. Don't close the jump ring.

4. Before closing the jump ring, add two jump rings with scales to the jump ring added in step 3. Close the jump ring.

5. Take one open jump ring and scoop up the jump ring added in step 4. Again, make sure that you have one jump ring with a scale to the left of the new open jump ring and one jump ring with a scale to the right of the new open jump ring. Before closing, add two jump rings with scales. Close the jump ring.

6. Repeat step 5 two more times.

7. Repeat steps 2–6 to make a second earring.

Design Option

This earring wire had three loops, so I added three separate scale dangles. These tiny scales are 12x7.6mm (.475x.3").

Peacock Blue Earrings

I made these earrings using the beautiful peacock blue color. But then
I thought, I can also make a pair for St. Patricks' Day using Kelly green
and white. I'm sure you can think of many other beautiful color
combinations! Let your imagination go wild!

» PREPARE: Open 30 jump rings. Close 6 jump rings.

Make the Earrings

materials
» **36** jump rings (peacock blue or Pacific blue enamel-coated copper)
» **1** pair earring wires (see "Making Earring Wires," p. 14)

tools
» **2** pairs chainnose, snubnose, flatnose, or bentnose pliers

1. Take one open jump ring and scoop up an earring wire and three closed jump rings. Close the jump ring.

2. Take a second open jump ring and repeat step 1, going through the three closed jump rings and the earring wire. Close the jump ring. (Some earring wires may not have enough space to add more than one jump ring. If this is the case, skip to step 4.)

3. Take a third open jump ring and repeat step 2. Close the jump ring.

4. Take one open jump ring and scoop up the three closed jump rings added in step 1. Close the jump ring.

5. Take a second open jump ring and repeat step 4. Close the jump ring.

6. Take a third open jump ring and repeat step 4. Close the jump ring.

7. Take one open jump ring and scoop up the three jump rings added in steps 4–6. Close the jump ring.

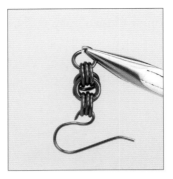

8. Take a second open jump ring and repeat step 7. Close the jump ring.

9. Take a third open jump ring and repeat step 7. Close the jump ring.

10. Take one open jump ring and scoop up the three jump rings added in steps 7–9. Close the jump ring.

11. Take a second open jump ring and repeat step 10. Close the jump ring.

12. Take a third open jump ring and repeat step 10. Close the jump ring.

13. Take one open jump ring and scoop up the three open jump rings added in steps 10–12. Close the jump ring.

Color Option

14. Take a second open jump ring and repeat step 13. Close the jump ring.

15. Take a third open jump ring and repeat step 13. Close the jump ring.

16. Make a second earring.

Box Chain Bracelet

This is quite a hefty bracelet in a glorious plum shade.
It would also make a nice gift for the man in your life,
if you use black or dark brown jump rings. You can
also make this bracelet from sterling silver and then
add a patina to darken it.

≫ PREPARE: Close 3 jump rings and open the remaining jump rings.

Make the Bracelet

materials

» **206** jump rings (plum enamel-coated copper)
» **1** clasp (see "Making a Clasp," p. 12)

tools

» **2** pairs chainnose, snubnose, flatnose, or bentnose pliers
» **1** twist tie
» **1** beading awl or a 2" piece of craft wire

1. Add three closed jump rings to a twist tie. From now on, wherever you add one jump ring, you will always add a second jump ring.

2. Take one open jump ring and scoop up the three closed jump rings added to the twist tie in step 1. Close the jump ring.

3. Take a second open jump ring and scoop up the three closed jump rings added to the twist tie in step 1. Close the jump ring.

4. Take one open jump ring and scoop up the two jump rings added in steps 2 and 3. Close the jump ring.

5. Take a second open jump ring and scoop up the two jump rings added in steps 2 and 3. Close the jump ring.

6. Hold your work by the three closed jump rings added to the twist tie in step 1. Fold down the two jump rings added in steps 4 and 5, one on either side of the two jump rings added in steps 2 and 3. Push the two folded down rings up, using your thumb and forefinger. As you can see, the two jump rings added in steps 2 and 3 will spread apart, exposing the two rings you flipped. Some of my students refer to this as "opening the duck's mouth and revealing his tongue."

7. I have inserted a yellow piece of wire showing where the next two jump rings will go. You can keep the wire there until you get your jump ring through.

8. Take one open jump ring and scoop up the two flipped jump rings from inside the duck's mouth. Close the jump ring.

9. Take a second open jump ring and repeat step 8. Close the jump ring.

10. Take one open jump ring and scoop up the two jump rings added in steps 8 and 9. Close the jump ring.

11. Take a second open jump ring and repeat step 10.

12. Repeat steps 6–11 until you reach the desired length of the bracelet.

13. Fold down the last two jump rings added from steps 10 and 11 and this time, instead of adding two jump rings, add three.

14. With one open jump ring, scoop up the three jump rings added in step 13. Before closing, add two closed jump rings. Close the jump ring.

15. With one open jump ring, scoop up the two closed jump rings added in step 14. Before closing, add two closed jump rings. Close the jump ring.

16. With one open jump ring, scoop up the two closed jump rings added in step 15. Before closing, add two closed jump rings. Close the jump ring.

17. If you made your own clasp like I did, follow these steps: Remove the twist tie from the three jump rings from step 1, open the loop on the clasp with a twisting motion (like when you open a jump ring), slip the three jump rings onto the clasp, and twist back the clasp.

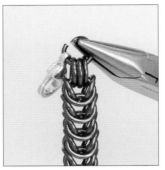

18. If you used a different type of clasp: Remove the twist tie from the three jump rings from step 1, and with one open jump ring, scoop up the three jump rings. Before closing, add the clasp. Close the jump ring.

Byzantine Three-Ring Möbius Earrings

As with the "Box Chain Bracelet," p. 33, you will also be
doing the flip in this weave. After making the last project,
you should have plenty of practice! These earrings also
incorporate a fun twist with a subtle möbius (or rosette).
I chose to make them relatively short, but you can
make them as long as you like, as in the color
variation on p. 39.

» PREPARE: Open all of the jump rings.

Make the Earrings

materials

» **34** jump rings (gold enamel-coated copper)
» **1** pair earring wires (gold-plated)

tools

» **2** pairs chainnose, snubnose, flatnose, or bentnose pliers
» **1** beading awl or a 2" piece of craft wire

1. Take one open jump ring and scoop up the earring wire. Close the jump ring.

2. Take one open jump ring and scoop up the jump ring added in step 1. Close the jump ring.

3. Take one open jump ring, scoop up the jump ring added in step 1, and go through the center of the jump ring added in step 2. Close the jump ring. The two rings will nest as shown.

4. Take one open jump ring and scoop up the jump ring added in step 1, go through the jump ring added in step 2, and also go through the jump ring added in step 3. Close the jump ring. You now have a three-ring rosette.

5. Take one open jump ring and pick up the three jump rings added in steps 2–4. You will be going right through the center of the rosette. Close the jump ring.

6. Take a second open jump ring and repeat step 5. Close the jump ring.

7. Take one open jump ring and scoop up the two jump rings added in steps 5 and 6. Close the jump ring.

8. Take a second open jump ring and repeat step 7. Close the jump ring.

Design Option To make these earrings, I repeated steps 5–21 to make them longer.

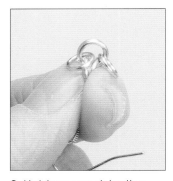   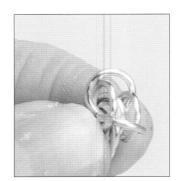

9. Hold your work by the rosette that you made in steps 2–4. Fold down the two jump rings added in steps 7 and 8, one on either side of the two jump rings added in steps 5 and 6. Push the two folded down rings up using your thumb and forefinger. As you can see, the two jump rings added in steps 7 and 8 will spread apart, exposing the two rings you flipped. Some of my students refer to this as "opening the duck's mouth and revealing his tongue."

10. I have inserted a beading awl (you can also use a 2" piece of craft wire) showing you where your next two jump rings will go. Keep the awl there until you get your jump ring through the proper jump rings.

11. Take one open jump ring and scoop up the two flipped jump rings from inside the duck's mouth. Close the jump ring.

12. Take a second open jump ring and repeat step 11. Close the jump ring.

13. Take a third open jump ring and repeat step 11. Close the jump ring.

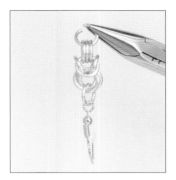

14. Take one open jump ring and scoop up the three jump rings added in steps 11–13. Close the jump ring.

15. Take a second open jump ring and repeat step 14. Close the jump ring.

16. Take one open jump ring and scoop up the two jump rings added in steps 14 and 15. Close the jump ring.

17. Take a second open jump ring and repeat step 16.

18. Fold down the two jump rings added in steps 16 and 17, one on either side of the two jump rings added in steps 14 and 15. Push the two folded down rings up using your thumb and forefinger. As you can see, the two jump rings added in steps 14 and 15 will spread apart, exposing the two rings you flipped.

19. Take one open jump ring and scoop up the two flipped jump rings from inside the duck's mouth. Close the jump ring.

20. Take a second open jump ring and repeat step 19. Before closing, go through the jump ring added in step 19. Close the jump ring.

21. Take a third open jump ring and repeat step 19. Before closing, go through both the jump ring added in step 19 and the jump ring added in step 20. Close the jump ring.

22. Repeat to make a second earring.

Byzantine Four-Ring Möbius Bracelet

I love this bracelet! It is substantial, delicate, and airy—all at the same time. It matches the "Byzantine Three-Ring Möbius Earrings," p. 37. Because I added the adjustable chain to the end of the bracelet, it will adjust from 7–7¾" long.

》PREPARE: Open 179 jump rings and close 3 jump rings.

Make the Bracelet

materials

》 **182** jump rings (silver enamel-coated copper)
》 **1** lobster-claw clasp
》 **1** charm

tools

》 **2** pairs chainnose, snubnose, flatnose, or bentnose pliers
》 **1** beading awl or a 2" piece of craft wire

1. Take one open jump ring and scoop up the lobster-claw clasp. Before closing, add three closed jump rings. Close the jump ring.

2. Take one open jump ring and scoop up the three closed jump rings added in step 1. Close the jump ring.

3. Take a second open jump ring and repeat step 2. Close the jump ring.

 The rings in the instructions are green because they are easier to see than silver.

4. Take one open jump ring and scoop up the two jump rings added in steps 2 and 3. Close the jump ring.

5. Take a second open jump ring and repeat step 4. Close the jump ring.

6. Hold your work by the three closed jump rings added in step 1. Fold down the two jump rings added in steps 4 and 5, one on either side of the two jump rings added in steps 2 and 3. Push the two folded-down jump rings up using your thumb and forefinger. As you can see, the two jump rings added in steps 2 and 3 will spread apart, exposing the two rings you flipped. Some of my students refer to this as "opening the duck's mouth and revealing his tongue."

7. I have inserted a beading awl (you can also use a piece of craft wire) showing you where the next two jump rings will go. Keep the awl there until you get the jump ring through.

8. Take one open jump ring and scoop up the two flipped jump rings from inside the duck's mouth. Close the jump ring.

9. Take a second open jump ring and repeat step 8. Before closing, go through the center of the jump ring added in step 8. Close the jump ring.

10. Take a third open jump ring and repeat step 8. Before closing, go through the center of the jump ring added in step 8 and the jump ring added in step 9. Close the jump ring. The three jump rings will "nest" into a three-ring möbius.

11. Take a fourth open jump ring and repeat step 8. Before closing, go through the center of the three-ring möbius. Close the jump ring. You will have to get the tips of your pliers very close to the split in the jump ring in order to close it. It is a very tight fit!

12. Take one open jump ring and pick up the four-ring möbius. Close the jump ring.

13. Take a second open jump ring and repeat step 12.

14. Take one open jump ring and scoop up the two jump rings added in steps 12 and 13. Close the jump ring.

15. Take a second open jump ring and repeat step 14.

16. Hold your work by the four-ring möbius added in steps 8–11. Fold down the two jump rings added in steps 14 and 15, one on either side of the two jump rings added in steps 12 and 13. Push the two folded down rings up using your thumb and forefinger. As you can see, the two jump rings added in steps 12 and 13 will spread apart, exposing the two rings you flipped.

17. I have inserted a beading awl showing you where your next two jump rings will go. Keep the awl there until you get your jump ring through the proper jump rings.

18. Take one open jump ring and scoop up the two flipped jump rings from inside the duck's mouth. Close the jump ring.

19. Take a second open jump ring and repeat step 18. Close the jump ring.

20. Take a third open jump ring and repeat step 18. Close the jump ring.

21. Repeat steps 2–20 ten times (or until you reach the desired length), then repeat steps 2–11. End your bracelet with a four-ring möbius.

22. I made a 1+1 chain of five single jump rings and attached it to the last jump rings. I also added a dragonfly charm to the end of my bracelet.

TIP **Before removing the beading awl, pinch the two flipped jump rings at their bottoms with your thumb and forefinger. Remove the beading awl, and you will be able to see exactly where to add the next two jump rings.**

Möbius Bracelet

If you completed the "Byzantine Four-Ring Möbius Bracelet,"
p. 42, this bracelet will be a breeze! I used two different colors, and
I encourage you to be creative. You will be surprised at what colors
actually do look good together. You don't need a color wheel; just
use the colors that you like!

» PREPARE: Open all of the jump rings.

Make the Bracelet

materials

- » **76** jump rings (peacock blue enamel-coated copper)
- » **76** jump rings (magenta enamel-coated copper)
- » **1** clasp (see "Making a Clasp," p. 12)

tools

- » **2** pairs chainnose, snubnose, flatnose, or bentnose pliers

1. Take one open peacock blue jump ring and scoop up the clasp. Close the jump ring.

2. Take one open magenta jump ring and scoop up the clasp. Close the jump ring. (If the loop on your clasp will only accommodate one jump ring, skip this step.)

3. Take one open peacock blue jump ring and scoop up both jump rings added in steps 1 and 2. Close the jump ring.

4. Take one open magenta jump ring, scoop up both jump rings added in steps 1 and 2, and go through the peacock blue jump ring added in step 3. Close the jump ring.

5. Take one open peacock blue jump ring, scoop up both jump rings added in steps 1 and 2, and go through the center of both the magenta jump ring added in step 4 and the peacock blue jump ring added in step 3. Close the jump ring.

6. Take one open magenta jump ring, scoop up both jump rings added in steps 1 and 2, and go through the peacock blue jump ring added in step 5, the magenta jump ring added in step 4, and the peacock blue jump ring added in step 3. Close the jump ring. The last three jump rings will "nest" together to form a four-ring möbius.

7. Take one open peacock blue jump ring and go through the center of the möbius from steps 3–6. Close the jump ring.

8. Repeat step 7 with a magenta jump ring. Close the jump ring.

9. Take one open peacock blue jump ring and scoop up both jump rings added in steps 7 and 8. Close the jump ring.

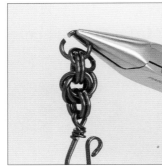

10. Take one open magenta jump ring, scoop up both jump rings added in steps 7 and 8, and go through the peacock blue jump ring added in step 9. Close the jump ring.

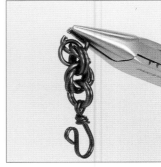

11. Take one open peacock blue jump ring, scoop up both jump rings added in steps 7 and 8, and go through both the magenta jump ring added in step 10 and the peacock blue jump ring added in step 9. Close the jump ring.

12. Take one open magenta jump ring, scoop up both jump rings added in steps 7 and 8, and go through the peacock blue jump ring added in step 11, the magenta jump ring added in step 10, and the peacock blue jump ring added in step 9. Close the jump ring.

13. Repeat steps 7–12 for the length of the bracelet.

14. Depending on the clasp you choose, you may want to end your bracelet with either one jump ring to hook the clasp into or two. You also have the option of making an adjustable clasp by adding a 2+2 chain (as seen on p. 48) to the end of your bracelet and adding a möbius to end the chain.

Color Option

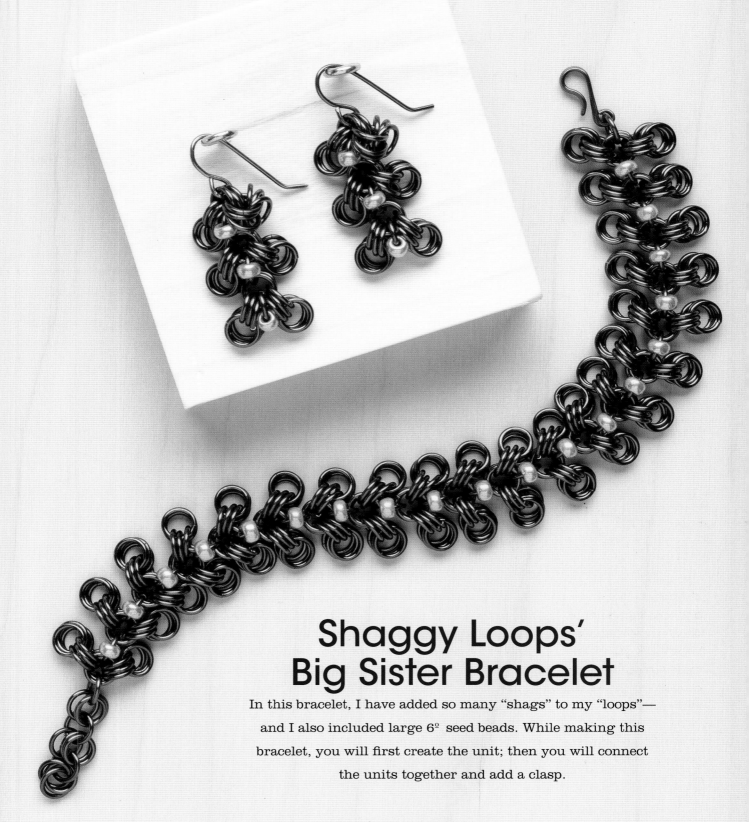

Shaggy Loops'
Big Sister Bracelet

In this bracelet, I have added so many "shags" to my "loops"—
and I also included large 6° seed beads. While making this
bracelet, you will first create the unit; then you will connect
the units together and add a clasp.

》 PREPARE: Close 126 jump rings. Open 187 jump rings.

Make the Units

materials

» **313** jump rings (gunmetal)
» **1** clasp (gunmetal)
» **19** 6º seed beads (very light gold metallic)

tools

» **2** pairs chainnose, snubnose, flatnose, or bentnose pliers

1. Take one open jump ring and scoop up three closed jump rings. Close the jump ring.

2. Take a second open jump ring and scoop up the three closed jump rings added in step 1. Close the jump ring.

3. Take a third open jump ring and scoop up the three closed jump rings added in step 1. Close the jump ring.

4. Take one open jump ring and scoop up the three open jump rings added in steps 1–3. Before closing the jump ring, add three closed jump rings. Close the jump ring.

5. Take a second open jump ring and scoop up the three open rings added in steps 1–3 and the three closed jump rings added in step 4. Close the jump ring.

6. Take a third open jump ring and scoop up the three open rings added in steps 1–3 and the three closed jump rings added in step 4. Close the jump ring.

7. Take one open jump ring and scoop up the three closed jump rings added in step 4. Close the jump ring.

8. Take a second open jump ring and scoop up the three closed jump rings added in step 4. Close the jump ring.

9. Take a third open jump ring and scoop up the three closed jump rings added in step 4. Close the jump ring.

10. Following steps 1–9, you have created one unit. Make 19 additional units for a total of 20 units.

Finish the Bracelet

11. Take one open jump ring and, in this order, add: one of the third set of three jump rings from one unit, a bead, and the third set of three jump rings from another unit. Close the jump ring.

12. Take one open jump ring and, in this order, add: one of the thirds sets of three jump rings from step 11, a bead, and the third set of three jump rings from another unit. Make sure that the bead ends up on the same side of the bracelet as in the previous step. Close the jump ring.

13. For an earring, stop here and add an earring wire. For a bracelet, continue connecting units together until you run out of units!

14. Take one open jump ring and scoop up the third set of three jump rings at one end of the bracelet. Before closing, add the clasp. Close the jump ring.

Add an Extender Chain

15. Take one open jump ring and scoop up the third set of three jump rings at the other end of the bracelet. Before closing, add three closed jump rings. Close the jump ring.

16. Take one open jump ring and scoop up the three closed jump rings added in step 15. Before closing, add three closed jump rings. Close the jump ring.

17. Take one open jump ring and scoop up the three closed jump rings added in step 16. Before closing, add three closed jump rings. Close the jump ring.

Beaded Four-Leaf Clover Bracelet

With this project, you will be combining Byzantine and möbius weaves.
I just love this color combination! For the alternate bracelet (p. 59), I
used classic silver-colored jump rings with red and white pearls. Don't
be afraid to experiment with your own unique color combinations.

» PREPARE: Open 67 jump rings and close 20 jump rings.

Make the Bracelet

materials

- » **87** jump rings (lemon enamel-coated)
- » **24"** of 18-gauge craft wire (lemon)
- » **1** clasp (see "Making a Clasp," p. 12)
- » **6** 8x10mm faceted AB beads (green)

tools

- » **2** pairs chainnose, snubnose, flatnose, or bentnose pliers
- » **1** beading awl or 2" piece of craft wire

1. Cut six 4" pieces of 18-gauge lemon craft wire.

 TIP

Measure one piece and then cut the remaining pieces from the first piece you measured and cut. Your pieces will be all the same length and it takes less time than measuring each piece individually.

2. Make six double-loop bead connectors with green beads (see "Making Double-Loop Bead Connectors," p. 16).

3. Take one open jump ring and scoop up two closed jump rings and one end of a connector. Close the jump ring.

4. Take a second open jump ring and scoop up the two closed jump rings added in step 3 and the connector from step 3. Close the jump ring. Set this connector aside.

5. Using a different connector, repeat steps 3 and 4.

6. Hold your work by the double loop of the connector added in step 3. Fold down the two closed jump rings added in step 3, one on either side of the two jump rings added in steps 3 and 4.

7. Push the two folded down jump rings up using your thumb and forefinger. As you can see, the two open jump rings added in steps 3 and 4 will spread apart, exposing the two closed rings you flipped. Some of my students refer to this as "opening the duck's mouth and revealing his tongue".

8. I have inserted a beading awl (you can use a 2" piece of craft wire) showing you where your next three jump rings will go. Keep the awl there and set aside.

9. Repeat steps 6 and 7 using the second connector from step 5. Take one open jump ring and scoop up the flipped jump rings (the duck's tongue).

10. Take the connector from step 8 (the one with the beading awl), remove the beading awl, and add it to the same open jump ring added in step 9. Close the jump ring.

11. Take a second open jump ring and repeat step 10. Close the jump ring.

12. Take a third open jump ring and repeat step 10. Close the jump ring.

   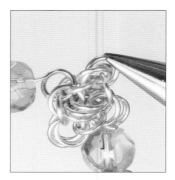

13. Working from one side, take one open jump ring and scoop up one of the jump rings added in step 3 and one of the jump rings added in step 5. Close the jump ring.

14. With one open jump ring, scoop up the same two jump rings you picked up in step 13 and also go through the open jump ring added in step 13. This will make a two-ring möbius.

15. Repeat step 14, this time going through both jump rings added in steps 13 and 14. Now you have a three-ring möbius.

16. Repeat steps 13–15 on the other side.

17. Take one open jump ring and scoop up the other end of the connector from step 8. Before closing, add two closed jump rings. Close the jump ring.

18. Take a second open jump ring and scoop up the two closed jump rings from step 17 and the connector from step 17. Close the jump ring.

19. Repeat steps 6–8 using the jump rings added in steps 17 and 18.

20. Take a new connector, and repeat steps 17 and 18. Take one open jump ring and scoop up the flipped jump rings (the duck's tongue).

 TIP

I used six connectors and five chain mail units, and my bracelet is approximately 6¾" long. Adjust the number of connectors and chain mail units as needed for the correct fit.

21. Take the connector from step 19 (the one with the beading awl), remove the beading awl, and add it to the same open jump ring added in step 20. Close the jump ring.

22. Take a second open jump ring and repeat step 21.

23. Take a third open jump ring and repeat step 21.

24. Repeat steps 13–16.

25. Repeat steps 17–24 using the remaining connectors.

26. Add your choice of clasp with a final jump ring.

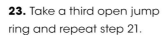

Color Option

Double Flower Earrings

These light-and-airy earrings are a breeze to make. Create them as long or short as you like! You will be making these earrings upside down until you get to step 6—the instructions are easier to follow that way.

» PREPARE: Close 24 jump rings. Open 26 jump rings.

Make the Earrings

materials

- **» 50** jump rings (purple enamel-coated copper)
- **» 1** pair earring wires (see "Making Earring Wires," p. 14)

tools

- **» 2** pairs chainnose, snubnose, flatnose, or bentnose pliers

 The rings in the instructions are purple because they are easier to see than silver.

1. Take one open jump ring and scoop up two closed jump rings and one earring wire. Close the jump ring.

2. Position the two closed jump rings added in step 1 and the open jump ring added in step 1 so you have "mouse ears" and a "forehead". Looking from left to right, the first jump ring is the mouse's left ear (a closed jump ring added in step 1), the center jump ring (an open jump ring added in step 1) is the mouse's forehead, and the third jump ring (the other closed jump ring added in step 1) is the mouse's right ear. Always make sure the mouse has a forehead.

3a. Take one open jump ring and working from the front, go down through the mouse's right ear.

3b. Go around the back of the mouse's forehead, and come up through the back of the mouse's left ear.

3c. Before closing the jump ring, add two closed jump rings. Close the jump ring.

4. Separate the two closed jump rings added in step 3c, making "mouse ears" and a "forehead". The bottoms of the jump rings added in step 3c should overlap the tops of the "ears" added in step 3.

5. Repeat steps 3a–4 four more times. Stop at step 3c.

6. Now, make two flowers: Starting on the right side and with one open jump ring, scoop up three jump rings. Close the jump ring.

7. Take one open jump ring and scoop up the next three jump rings. Close the jump ring.

8. Flip the earring over and repeat steps 6 and 7.

 TIP

With this weave, do not lay your work down while making mouse ears—but if you do, make sure all of your foreheads are pointing in the same direction.

9. Add a möbius to the bottom center jump ring: Take one open jump ring, and scoop up the center jump ring. Close the jump ring.

10. Take a second open jump ring, scoop up the same bottom jump ring from step 9 and go through the open jump ring added in step 9. Close the jump ring.

11. Take a third open jump ring, scoop up the same bottom jump ring from step 9, and go through both the jump rings added in steps 9 and 10. Close the jump ring.

Double Flower Bracelet

The European 4-in-1 weave is among the oldest chain mail weaves. It was used to make armor back in 400 B.C. This bracelet starts out as a typical European weave and gets fancy with some "flowers" on the sides. I find it very delicate and lacy.

>> PREPARE: Close 120 jump rings. Open 104 jump rings.

Make a Strip of European 4-in-1

materials

» **224** jump rings (silver blue enamel-coated copper)
» **1** 5-ring slide clasp

tools

» **2** pairs chainnose, snubnose, flatnose, or bentnose pliers
» **2** twist ties

1. Put a closed jump ring on a twist tie.

 TIP **This bracelet fits a 6½" wrist. Each two section unit measures ⅝". I suggest adding one two unit set and then re-measuring.**

2. With one open jump ring, scoop up two closed jump rings and the jump ring you added in step 1. Close the jump ring.

3. Position the two closed jump rings added in step 2 and the jump ring added in step 2 so you have "mouse ears" and a "forehead". Looking from left to right, the first jump ring is the mouse's left ear (a closed jump ring added in step 2), the center jump ring (the open jump ring added in step 2) is the mouse's forehead, and the third jump ring (the other closed jump ring added in step 2) is the mouse's right ear. Always make sure the mouse has a forehead.

4a. With an open jump ring and working from the front, go down through the mouse's right ear.

4b. Go around the back of the mouse's forehead, and come up through the back of the mouse's left ear.

4c. Before closing the jump ring, add two closed jump rings. Close the jump ring.

5. Separate the two closed jump rings added in step 4c, making "mouse ears" and a "forehead". The bottoms of the jump rings added in step 4c should overlap the tops of the "ears" added in step 2.

6. Repeat steps 4a–4c.

7. Repeat steps 5 and 6 for the desired length of the bracelet.

8. Set that strip aside and begin a new strip, repeating steps 1–7.

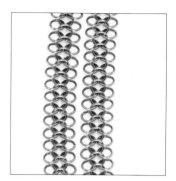

9. Place the two strips of European 4-in-1 side by side with their foreheads pointing up.

TIP **You have completed two separate strips of European 4-in-1 weave. Now you will join the two strips together. Later, you will finish each side with the flowers.**

Join the Strips

10. Now, you will join the strips together up the center: With one open jump ring, pick up three jump rings from the right side of the first strip and three jump rings from the left side of the second strip. Close the jump ring. (Start from the bottom in case you need to add more rings at the top.)

11. Repeat step 10, using the next three jump rings from the right side of the first strip and the next three jump rings from the left side of the second strip.

12. Repeat step 11 all the way to the top of the strips. Add more mouse ears as need to have multiples of threes.

13. Now, you will add the flowers down each side of the bracelet: Starting on the right side of the right strip, with one open jump ring, scoop up three jump rings. Close the jump ring.

Finish the Bracelet

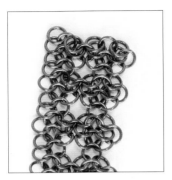

14. Repeat step 13 and continue down the right side of the bracelet, each time picking up the next three jump rings with one open jump ring.

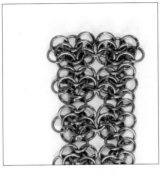

15. Flip the bracelet over and repeat steps 13 and 14 to the bottom of the bracelet.

16. Now, add the clasp. (I used blue jump rings to show you where the connections to the clasp will be.) You may notice that the middle loop of the clasp is attached to a jump ring that has not been added yet. You will add that jump ring in the next step.

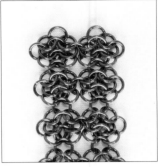

17. Remove the two jump rings with the twist ties attached. These two jump rings will become two of the three jump rings used to attach the clasp. Notice these two jump rings only go through two other jump rings. This will be important when you attach the clasp to the other side. You will need to add a third jump ring in the middle.

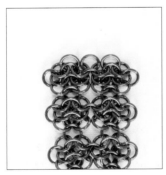

18. First, make sure all of the foreheads are pointing up. (I used red jump rings to show you where to place the next set of jump rings.) With one open jump ring, scoop up the left ear from the strip on the right and the right ear from the left strip. Close the jump ring. This jump ring will only go through two jump rings.

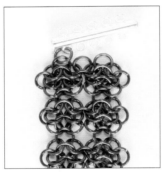

19. Working from left to right on the clasp, with one open jump ring, scoop up the forehead from the left strip and also scoop up the leftmost loop on the clasp. Close the jump ring.

20. With one open jump ring, scoop up the forehead from the left strip and also scoop up the second loop from the left loop on the clasp. Close the jump ring.

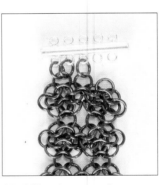

21. With one open jump ring, scoop up the jump ring you added in step 18 and scoop up the third or center loop on the clasp. Close the jump ring.

22. With one open jump ring, scoop up the forehead from the right strip and also scoop up the fourth loop from the left on the clasp. Close the jump ring.

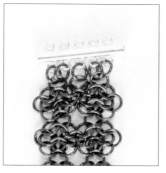

23. With one open jump ring, scoop up the forehead from the right strip and also scoop up the fifth loop from the left on the clasp. Close the jump ring.

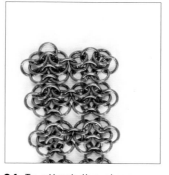

24. To attach the clasp to the other end, you will need to attach three new jump rings. First, make sure all of the foreheads are pointing up. Working on the left strip first, make one forehead using the last two ears: With an open jump ring and working from the front, go down through the mouse's right ear, around the back of the mouse's forehead, and come up through the back of the mouse's left ear. Close the jump ring.

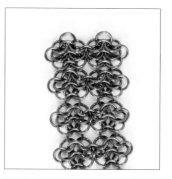

25. Repeat step 24 on the right strip.

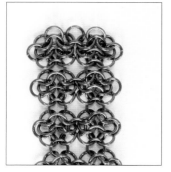

26. Repeat step 18.

27. Repeat steps 19–23.

TIP

Leave the clasp closed when attaching both ends of the clasp to the bracelet. This will make certain the orientation of the clasp is correct and the bracelet does not get twisted.

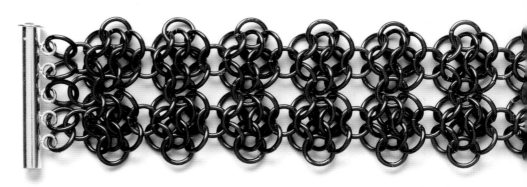

Rosebuds Bracelet

An unusual color combination results in unexpected beauty in this substantial bracelet. I chose these shades of green and pink because the three interlocked rose gold jump rings look like rose buds on top of healthy, green leaves. At first glance, this bracelet may seem intimidating, but you have done all of these steps in the previous projects.

» PREPARE: Close 96 green jump rings and open 51 green jump rings. Open all of the rose gold jump rings.

Start with the Green Jump Rings

materials
- » **147** jump rings (kelly green)
- » **105** jump rings (rose gold)
- » **1** clasp (see "Making a Clasp," p. 12)

tools
- » **2** pairs chainnose, snubnose, flatnose, or bentnose pliers
- » **1** twist tie

 TIP

Always make sure the mouse has a forehead, if the mouse has no mouse ears, flip the weave over.

1. Take one open green jump ring and scoop up the clasp. Close the jump ring.

2. Take a second open jump ring and scoop up the clasp. Close the jump ring.

3. Take one open jump ring and scoop up the two open jump rings added in steps 1 and 2. Before closing, add two closed jump rings. Close the jump ring.

4. Position the two closed jump rings at the end of the chain so you have "mouse ears" and a "forehead". Looking from left to right, the first jump ring is the mouse's left ear (a closed jump rings added in step 3), the center jump ring (the open jump ring added in step 3) is the mouse's forehead, and the third jump ring (the other closed jump ring added in step 3) is the mouse's right ear.

5a. Take one open green jump ring and working from the front, go down through the mouse's right ear.

b. Go around the back of the mouse's forehead, and come up through the back of the mouse's left ear.

c. Before closing the jump ring, add two green closed jump rings. Close the jump ring.

6. Separate the two closed jump rings added in step 5c, making "mouse ears" and a "forehead". The bottoms of the jump rings added in step 5c should overlap the tops of the "ears" added in step 3.

7. Repeat steps 5a–5c.

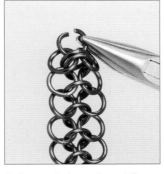

8. Repeat steps 6 and 7 42 times. (The bracelet will shrink significantly once you have added all the rose buds, so keep that in mind.)

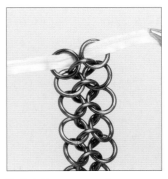

9. Add two green jump rings to the last set of mouse ears. Insert the twist tie into the two green jump rings.

Add the Rose Gold Jump Rings

10. Starting at the clasp end and working on the right side, take one open rose gold jump ring and scoop up three green mouse ears. Close the jump ring.

11. Take one open rose gold jump ring and scoop up the next three green mouse ears. Close the jump ring.

12. Repeat step 11 all the way to the end. You may need to add or subtract green jump rings at the end.

13. Flip the bracelet over and start again on the right side with the clasp at the top: Take one open rose gold jump ring and scoop up the first three green mouse ears. Close the jump ring.

14. Repeat step 13 all the way to the end.

15. Now you will join the rose gold jump rings together and make the rose buds: Starting at the clasp end, take one open rose gold jump ring and scoop up both the left rose gold jump ring and the right rose gold jump ring. Close the jump ring.

16. Take a second open rose gold jump ring and scoop up the same two rose gold jump rings scooped up in step 15. Before closing the jump ring, go through the rose gold jump ring added in step 15. Close the jump ring.

17. Take a third open rose gold jump ring and scoop up the same two rose gold jump rings scooped up in step 15. Before closing the jump ring, go through the rose gold jump ring added in step 16 and the rose gold jump ring added in step 15. Close the jump ring.

18. Repeat steps 15–17 for all the remaining rose gold jump rings. You will have 15 rose buds.

19. Take one open green jump ring and scoop up the two green jump rings added in step 9. Before closing, add two closed green jump rings. Close the jump ring.

20. Take one open green jump ring and scoop up the two closed green jump rings added in step 19. Before closing, add two closed green jump rings. Close the jump ring.

21. Take one open green jump ring and scoop up the two closed green jump rings added in step 20. Before closing, add two closed green jump rings. Close the jump ring.

   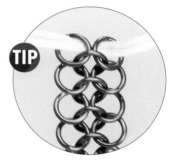

22. Optional: You may want to change the orientation of the clasp. Simply remove the clasp from the green jump ring added in step 1 and re-close the jump ring.

23. Take one open jump ring and scoop up the clasp and the open green jump ring added in step 1. Close the jump ring.

24. Take a second open green jump ring and repeat step 23. Use the single green jump rings to hook the clasp.

If you are going to lay your bracelet down, take a twist tie and put it in the path that you will be using for the next jump ring. This will keep the jump rings from twisting on you.

 Tugging on the clasp will make those jump rings fall into place!

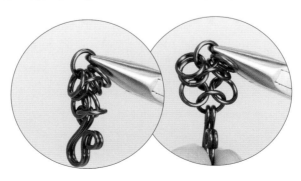

Angel Wings Bracelet

At first glance, this bracelet looks complicated to make—but when
you break it down, it is very simple. I love the way it looks like
angel's wings. Try different types of metals and mix up the beads
to make this bracelet truly your own.

» PREPARE: Open 158 jump rings. Close 2 jump rings.

Make the Bracelet

materials

- **» 160** jump rings (gunmetal)
- **» 1** lobster claw clasp (gunmetal)
- **» 48** 6º seed beads (very light gold metallic)

tools

- **» 2** pairs chainnose, snubnose, flatnose, or bentnose pliers

1. Take one open jump ring and scoop up two closed jump rings and one end of the clasp. Close the jump ring.

2. String a bead on one open jump ring and add the open jump ring to one of the two closed jump rings added in step 1. Close the jump ring.

3. String a bead on one open jump ring and add the open jump ring to the other closed jump ring added in step 1. Close the jump ring.

4. Add one open jump ring to the two closed jump rings added in step 1. Close the jump ring.

5. Flip the beaded rings over and add one open jump ring to the two closed jump rings added in step 1. Close the jump ring.

6. You will have a sandwich of one closed jump ring, the two jump rings with beads, and another closed jump ring.

7. Working the left side of the weave, with an open jump ring, pick up the jump ring added in step 4, the jump ring with the bead added in step 2, and the jump ring added in step 5. Close the jump ring. Make sure the beads are on the outside of the jump rings.

8. Flip the beaded rings over and repeat step 7.

9. String a bead on one open jump ring and add the open jump ring to the jump ring added in step 7. Close the jump ring.

10. String a bead on one open jump ring and add the open jump ring to the jump ring added in step 8. Close the jump ring.

11. Add one open jump ring to the two jump rings added in steps 7 and 8. Close the jump ring.

12. Flip the weave over and add one open jump ring to the two jump rings added in steps 7 and 8. Close the jump ring. You are making another sandwich (see step 6)!

13. Repeat steps 7–12 until you reach the desired length of the bracelet.

14. Separately, make a 1+1 chain of approximately six jump rings. Add one open jump ring to the two jump rings at the end of the bracelet. Before closing the jump ring, add the chain you just made. Close the jump ring.

Butterfly Wings Bracelet

This bracelet reminds me of delicate wings beating on sunshiny winds. It's easy to make, but the color and composition of the piece are stunning. This is a nice reminder of summer on your wrist!

» PREPARE: Open all of the jump rings.

Make the Bracelet

materials

» **166** jump rings (rose or hot pink enamel-coated copper

» **1** clasp (see "Making a Clasp," p. 12)

tools

» **2** pairs chainnose, snubnose, flatnose, or bentnose pliers

1. Take one open jump ring and scoop up the clasp. Close the jump ring.

2. Take a second open jump ring and repeat step 1.

3. Take one open jump ring and scoop up the two jump rings attached to the clasp. Close the jump ring.

4. Take a second open jump ring and repeat step 3.

5. Take one open jump ring and scoop up the two jump rings added in step 3 and 4. Close the jump ring.

6. Take a second open jump ring and repeat step 5.

7. Make mouse ears with the two jump rings added in steps 5 and 6. (Refer to the "Rosebuds Bracelet," p. 68, for a full explanation.)

8. With one open jump ring, go down through the mouse's right ear from step 5 and around the back of the mouse's forehead.

9. Go up through the mouse's left ear added in step 6. Close the jump ring.

10. Repeat steps 8 and 9 with a second open jump ring.

11. Take one open jump ring and scoop up the two jump rings added in steps 8–10. Close the jump ring.

12. Take a second open jump ring and repeat step 11.

13. Make mouse ears with the two jump rings added in steps 11 and 12.

14. Take one open jump ring, go down through the mouse's right ear from step 11, and go around the back of the mouse's forehead.

15. Go up through the mouse's left ear added in step 12. Close the jump ring.

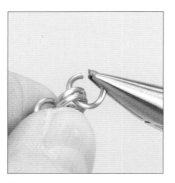

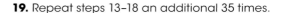

16. Take one open jump ring and repeat steps 14 and 15.

17. Take one open jump ring and scoop up the two jump rings added in steps 14–16. Close the jump ring.

18. Take a second open jump ring and repeat step 17.

19. Repeat steps 13–18 an additional 35 times.

20. To make the bracelet adjustable: Instead of making mouse ears out of the last two jump rings added, add two open jump rings to those jump rings. Close the jump rings.

21. Add two open jump rings to the two jump rings added in step 20. Close the jump rings.

22. Add two open jump rings to the two jump rings added in step 21. Close the jump rings.

23. Add two open jump rings to the two jump rings added in step 22. Close the jump rings.

24. Add two open jump rings to the two jump rings added in step 23. Close the jump rings.

Red, White, and Blue Möbius Earrings

OK, so I'm obsessed with the birth of my country! I love the combination of red, white, and blue. These earrings are not just for the Fourth of July, but for anytime they match your outfit. You could even wear them when you go to vote!

>> PREPARE: Open all of the jump rings.

materials

» **10** jump rings (red enamel-coated copper)
» **10** jump rings (white enamel-coated copper)
» **10** jump rings (blue enamel-coated copper)
» **1** pair earring wires (see "Making Earring Wires," p. 14)

tools

» **2** pairs chainnose, snubnose, flatnose, or bentnose pliers

Make the Earrings

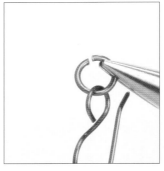

1. Take one open red jump ring and scoop up one earring wire. Close the jump ring.

2. Take one open white jump ring, and scoop up the earring wire and the red jump ring added in step 1. Close the jump ring.

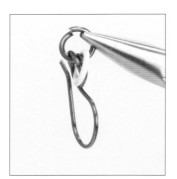

3. Take one open blue jump ring and scoop up the earring wire, the red jump ring added in step 1, and the white jump ring added in step 2. Close the jump ring.

4. Take one red open jump ring and scoop up the red, white, and blue jump rings added in steps 1–3. Close the jump ring. The intertwining of the three jump rings is called a möbius.

5. Take one white open jump ring and scoop up the red, white, and blue möbius and the red jump ring added in step 4. Close the jump ring.

6. Take one blue open jump ring and scoop up the red, white, and blue möbius and the red and white jump rings added in steps 4 and 5. Close the jump ring.

7. Repeat steps 4–6 three more times.

8. Repeat to make a second earring.

Color
Option

Möbius Barrel Weave Bracelet

I bet you never thought orchid, rose, and peacock blue would

result in such a beautiful combination! This lovely mix of colors

reminds me of a peacock's feathers.

>> PREPARE: Open all of the pink and blue jump rings. Open 27 purple jump rings and close 40 purple jump rings.

Make the Bracelet

materials

- » **67** jump rings (orchid purple enamel-coated copper)
- » **22** jump rings (rose pink enamel-coated copper)
- » **22** jump rings (peacock blue enamel-coated copper)
- » **1** clasp (see "Making a Clasp," p. 12)

tools

- » **2** pairs chainnose, snubnose, flatnose, or bentnose pliers

1. Take one open purple jump ring and scoop up the clasp. Close the jump ring.

2. Take a second open purple jump ring and repeat step 1.

3. Notice that the jump ring on the left is underneath the jump ring on the right and that they overlap in the middle. Where they overlap is called the "eye". See how it kind of looks like a sideways cat's eye? You will go *around* the eye with two jump rings.

4. Take one open pink jump ring and go down through the front of the right jump ring and then around the back of the eye and up through the back of the left jump ring. Close the jump ring.

5. Repeat step 4 with a blue jump ring, but before closing the jump ring, go through the pink jump ring. Close the jump ring.

Color
Option

6. The next purple jump ring will be going through the top of the eye above the two jump rings added in steps 4 and 5.

7. Take one open purple jump ring and go through the top of the eye. Before closing, add two closed purple jump rings. Close the jump ring.

8. Repeat steps 4–7 20 more times, ending at step 5.

9. Take one open purple jump ring and go through the top of the eye. Close the jump ring.

10. Link four purple jump rings together in a 1+1 chain. Before closing the fourth purple jump ring, scoop up the open purple jump ring added in step 9. Close the jump ring.

11. Take one open pink jump ring, scoop up the third link in the chain, and go through the fourth link in the chain. Close the jump ring.

12. Repeat step 11 with one open blue jump ring by going through the third and fourth link in the chain. Before closing, go through the pink ring added in step 11. Close the jump ring.

TIP

You want the two purple jump rings that make up the eye to be consistent. In this case, the left jump ring is always behind the right jump ring. If you prefer the right jump ring to be behind the left jump ring, make sure that you keep to that pattern.

Three-Ring Barrel Bracelet

For this bracelet, I wanted to use two different precious metal colors for the jump rings. I am hoping this will make it clearer to see where each jump ring will be. Like most chain mail weaves, one set of instructions are repeated over and over again. This repetition will help to solidify the weave in your mind and make the bracelet easier to contruct as you go along.

» PREPARE: Open 60 gold jump rings and close 6 gold jump rings. Open 22 silver jump rings and close 40 silver jump rings.

Make the Bracelet

materials

- **» 66** jump rings (gold enamel-coated copper)
- **» 62** jump rings (silver enamel-coated copper
- **» 1** lobster-claw clasp

tools

- **» 2** pairs chainnose, snubnose, flatnose, or bentnose pliers

1. Take one open silver jump ring and scoop up the clasp. Close the jump ring.

2. Take one open silver jump ring and scoop up the silver jump ring added in step 1. Before closing the jump ring, add two closed silver jump rings. Close the jump ring.

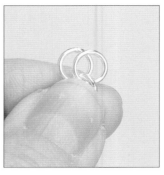

3. Notice that the jump ring on the left is underneath the jump ring on the right and that they overlap in the middle. Where they overlap is called the "eye." See how it kind of looks like a sideways cat's eye? You will go around the eye with two jump rings.

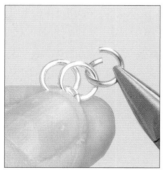

4. Take one open gold jump ring and go down through the front of the right jump ring, around the back of the eye, and up through the back of the left jump ring. Close the jump ring.

5. Take a second gold jump ring and repeat step 4.

6. Take a third gold jump ring and repeat step 4.

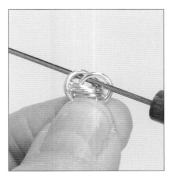

7. The next silver jump ring will be going through the top of the eye above the three gold jump rings added in steps 4–6.

8. Take one open silver jump ring and go through the top of the eye. Before closing, add two closed silver jump rings. Close the jump ring.

9. Place the right closed silver jump ring on top of the left closed silver jump ring, forming an eye.

10. Take one open gold jump ring and encircle the eye. Close the jump ring.

11. Take a second open gold jump ring and repeat step 10. Close the jump ring.

12. Take a third open gold jump ring and repeat step 10. Close the jump ring.

13. Repeat steps 8–12 18 times for a total of 20 three-ring barrels. On the last barrel (step 8), instead of adding two closed silver jump rings, add three closed gold jump rings. Close the jump ring.

14. Take one open silver jump ring and scoop up the three closed gold jump rings added in step 13. Before closing, add three closed gold jump rings. Close the jump ring.

Double Spiral Bracelet

To make this bracelet more interesting, I used enamel-coated rose gold jump rings separated by magenta jump rings in a repeating pattern of twos and threes. What do you think? Does it add drama? Try different combinations and colors to make this bracelet your own.

» PREPARE: Close 2 magenta jump rings. Open all of the remaining jump rings.

Make the Bracelet

materials

» **107** jump rings (rose gold enamel-coated copper)
» **57** jump rings (magenta enamel-coated copper)
» **1** lobster claw clasp

tools

» **2** pairs chainnose, snubnose, flatnose, or bentnose pliers

1. Make a 1+1 chain of one rose gold jump ring, one magenta jump ring, one rose gold jump ring, and one magenta jump ring.

2. Take one open rose gold jump ring and scoop up the last magenta jump ring added in step 1. Before closing, add two closed magenta jump rings. Close the jump ring.

3. Take one open rose gold jump ring and go through the single rose gold jump ring added in step 2 and the two closed magenta jump rings added in step 2. Close the jump ring.

4. Take one open rose gold jump ring and repeat step 3, making sure not to cross over the rose gold jump ring added in step 3.

5. Take one open magenta jump ring and go through the two rose gold jump rings added in steps 3 and 4 and the two closed magenta jump rings added in step 2. Close the jump ring.

6. Take one open magenta jump ring and repeat step 5.

7. Take one open rose gold jump ring and go through the two rose gold jump rings added in steps 3 and 4 and the two magenta jump rings added in steps 5 and 6. Close the jump ring.

8. Take one open rose gold jump ring and repeat step 7.

9. Take one open rose gold jump ring and go through the two magenta jump rings added in steps 5 and 6 and through the two rose gold jump rings added in steps 7 and 8. Close the jump ring.

10. Take one open rose gold jump ring and repeat step 9.

11. Take one open magenta jump ring and go through the two rose gold jump rings added in steps 7 and 8 and the two rose gold jump rings added in steps 9 and 10. Close the jump ring.

12. Take one open magenta jump ring and repeat step 11.

13. Take one open rose gold jump ring and go through the two rose gold jump rings added in steps 9 and 10 and the two magenta jump rings added in steps 11 and 12. Close the jump ring.

14. Take one open rose gold jump ring and repeat step 13.

15. Take one open rose gold jump ring and go through the two magenta jump rings added in steps 11 and 12 and the two rose gold jump rings added in steps 13 and 14. Close the jump ring.

16. Take one rose gold jump ring and repeat step 15.

17. Take one open rose gold jump ring and go through the two rose gold jump rings added in steps 13 and 14 and the two rose gold jump rings added in steps 15 and 16. Close the jump ring.

18. Take one rose gold jump ring and repeat step 17.

 TIP

At this point, you should have a chain of five jump rings followed by two magenta jump rings, two rose gold jump rings, two magenta jump rings, two rose gold jump rings, two rose gold jump rings, two magenta jump rings, two rose gold jump rings, two rose gold jump rings, and two rose gold jump rings. You will be starting the pattern over again with steps 19 and 20.

19. Take an open magenta jump ring and go through the two rose gold jump rings added in steps 15 and 16 and the two rose gold jump rings added in steps 17 and 18. Close the jump ring.

20. Take one magenta jump ring and repeat step 19.

21. Repeat steps 3–20 until you reach the desired length of the bracelet.

22. If you ended your bracelet with two magenta jump rings (like I did), use one rose gold jump ring to attach the lobster-claw clasp. If you ended your bracelet with two rose gold jump rings, use one magenta jump ring to attach the clasp.

 TIP

You may need to open your jump rings a bit larger than normal to make it easier to pick up the four jump rings.

Möbius Ears Bracelet

This bracelet is more substantial than a "traditional" European 4-in-1 chain mail weave. For extra interest, I added an "ear" on each edge (which makes it a two-ring möbius).

»PREPARE: Close 86 jump rings. Open all the remaining jump rings.

Start the Weave

materials

» **225** jump rings (aqua or teal enamel-coated copper)
» **1** clasp (see "Making a Clasp," p. 12)

tools

» **2** pairs chainnose, snubnose, flatnose, or bentnose pliers
» **1** twist tie or large paperclip

1. Take one open jump ring, and scoop up the clasp. Close the jump ring.

2. Take a second open jump ring and repeat step 1.

3. Take one open jump ring (soon to be the mouse's "forehead") and scoop up the two jump rings added in steps 1 and 2. Before closing, add two closed jump rings (these two rings will become the mouse's "ears"). Close the jump ring.

4. Take one open jump ring and scoop up the open jump ring added in step 3 (the mouse's forehead) and one of the closed jump rings added in step 3 (making one möbius ear). Close the jump ring.

5. Take a second open jump ring and repeat step 4, this time scooping up the second closed jump ring added in step 3 (making a second möbius ear). Close the jump ring.

6. Position the two möbiused ears jump rings added in steps 3–5 and the open jump ring (mouse's forehead) added in step 3 so you have mouse ears and a forehead.

 TIP

Looking from left to right, the first jump rings (the möbius) are the mouse's left ear, the center jump ring (the open jump ring added in step 3) is the mouse's forehead, and the right jump rings (the second möbius) are the mouse's right ear. Always make sure the mouse has a forehead. Turn your work over and you will see that there is no forehead.

7. Take one open jump ring (mouse's next forehead) and working from the front, go down through the mouse's right ears, around the back of the mouse's forehead, and come up through the back of the mouse's left ears. Before closing, add two closed jump rings. Close the jump ring.

8. Take one open jump ring and go through the forehead added in step 7 and through the jump ring on the left (mouse's left ear). Close the jump ring.

9. Take a second open jump ring and repeat step 8, only this time, go through the jump ring on the right (mouse's right ear). Close the jump ring.

Design Option

I love mixing gold and silver rings. I think the combination looks very elegant—and it goes with everything!

10. Position the jump rings so you have two left ears (möbius), a forehead, and two right ears (möbius).

11. Repeat steps 7–10 an additional 41 times.

Finish the Bracelet

12. Now you will add the extension chain. Take one open jump ring and scoop up the last forehead you made. Close the jump ring.

13. Take one open jump ring and scoop up the open jump ring added in step 12. Close the jump ring.

14. Take one open jump ring and scoop up the open jump ring added in step 13. Close the jump ring.

15. Take one open jump ring and scoop up the open jump ring added in step 14. Close the jump ring.

16. We will now make what is called a four jump-ring möbius. Take one open jump ring and scoop up the open jump ring added in step 15. Close the jump ring.

17. Take one open jump ring and scoop up the open jump ring added in step 15 and the open jump ring added in step 16. Close the jump ring.

18. Take one open jump ring and scoop up the open jump ring added in step 15, the open jump ring added in step 16, and the open jump ring added in step 17. Close the jump ring.

19. Take one open jump ring and scoop up the open jump ring added in step 15, the open jump ring added in step 16, the open jump ring added in step 17, and the open jump ring added in step 18. Close the jump ring.

 While you're adding mouse ears, do not lay your work down. If you do, make sure all of your foreheads are pointing up. You could also put a wire or twist tie through the space where the next jump ring will be added.

Purple Cross Earrings

When I originally designed these earrings, I had them inverted. I
showed them to my husband and he suggested flipping them over.
Voilà! Gorgeous cross earrings!

» PREPARE: Open 44 jump rings. Close 24 jump rings.

Make the Earrings

materials

» **68** jump rings (orchid or purple enamel-coated copper)
» **1** pair earring wires (see "Making Earring Wires," p. 14)

tools

» **2** pairs chainnose, snubnose, flatnose, or bentnose pliers
» **1** twist tie or large paperclip

1. Add three closed jump rings to a twist tie or paperclip.

2. Take one open jump ring and scoop up the three closed jump rings on the twist tie or paperclip. Before closing the jump ring, add two closed jump rings. Close the jump ring.

3. Take a second open jump ring and run it through the same path as the open jump ring added in step 2. Close the jump ring.

4. Fold down the two closed jump rings added in step 2.

5. Spread open the two open jump rings added in steps 2 and 3.

6. Take one open jump ring and scoop up from the inside of the two open jump rings added in steps 2 and 3, the two closed jump rings added in step 2. Close the jump ring.

7. Take a second open jump ring and repeat step 6.

8. Take a third open jump ring and repeat step 6. Close the jump ring.

9. Take one open jump ring and scoop up the three open jump rings added in steps 6–8. Before closing, add three closed jump rings. Close the jump ring.

10. Take one open jump ring and scoop up the open jump ring added in step 9. Close the jump ring.

11. Take a second open jump ring and repeat step 10. Close the jump ring.

12. Take a third open jump ring and repeat step 10. Close the jump ring.

13. You should now have a total of nine jump rings on the one open jump ring added in step 9.

14. Take one open jump ring and scoop up the three closed jump rings added in step 9. Before closing the jump ring, add two closed jump rings. Close the jump ring.

15. Take a second open jump ring and go through the same path as the jump ring in step 14. Close the jump ring.

16. Take one open jump ring and repeat steps 4–6. Close the jump ring.

17. Take a second open jump ring and repeat steps 4–6. Close the jump ring.

18. Take a third open jump ring and repeat step 6. Close the jump ring.

19. Take one open jump ring and scoop up the three remaining jump rings (the three open jump rings added in steps 10–12) on the jump ring added in step 9. Before closing, add two closed jump rings. Close the jump ring.

20. Take a second open jump ring and go through the same path as the jump ring in step 19. Close the jump ring.

21. Take one open jump ring and repeat steps 4–6. Close the jump ring.

22. Take a second open jump ring and repeat step 6. Close the jump ring.

23. Take a third open jump ring and repeat steps 4–6. Close the jump ring.

24. You will now join the two units you just made and add the earring wire: Take one open jump ring and scoop up both inside folded down closed jump rings from steps 14 and 19. Before closing, add the earring wire. Close the jump ring.

25. Take a second open jump ring and go through the same path as the jump ring in step 24.

26. Take a third open jump ring and go through the same path as the jump ring in step 24.

27. Remove the twist tie or paperclip from the bottom of the earring.

28. Repeat to make a second earring.

Color Option

Crystal Gold Earrings

I bought these gorgeous Swarovski crystal drops and knew I had
to make them into an elegant pair of earrings. The gold jump
rings really make the crystals pop!

» PREPARE: Open all of the jump rings.

Make the Earrings

materials

» **14** jump rings (gold enamel-coated copper)
» **2** 6mm Swarovski round crystal drops (17704, crystal)
» **1** pair earring wires

tools

» **2** pairs chainnose, snubnose, flatnose, or bentnose pliers

1. Take one open jump ring and scoop up earring wire. Close the jump ring.

2. Take one open jump ring and scoop up the jump ring added in step 1. Close the jump ring.

3. Take one open jump ring and scoop up the jump ring added in step 1. Go through the jump ring added in step 2. Close the jump ring.

4. Take one open jump ring and scoop up the jump ring added in step 1. Go through the jump ring added in step 2 and the jump ring added in step 3. Close the jump ring.

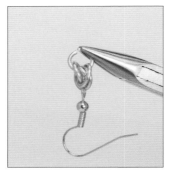

5. Take one open jump ring and scoop up the jump ring added in step 1 and go through the jump ring added in step 2, the jump ring added in step 3, and the jump ring added in step 4. Close the jump ring.

6. Take one open jump ring and scoop up the jump ring added in step 1. Go through the jump ring added in step 2, the jump ring added in step 3, the jump ring added in step 4, and the jump ring added in step 5. Close the jump ring.

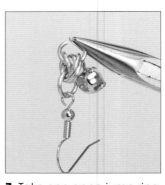

7. Take one open jump ring and go through the center of the five-ring möbius you just made. Before closing the jump ring, string the crystal chaton. Close the jump ring.

8. Repeat to make a second earring.

Beaded Four-Leaf Clover Earrings

I had so much fun making the "Beaded Four-Leaf Clover Bracelet,"
p. 55, I thought I would also make a pair of earrings! If you
want a different look, try making the earrings using pearls and
silver-colored jump rings, as in the variation on p. 106. You can
also use different-sized beads and even crystals for extra sparkle!

materials

- » **40** jump rings (lemon)
- » 8" 18-gauge craft wire (lemon)
- » **6** 8x10mm faceted beads (AB green)
- » **1** pair earring wires (see "Making Earring Wires," p. 14)

tools

- » **2** pairs chainnose, snubnose, flatnose, or bentnose pliers
- » **1** beading awl or a 2" piece of craft wire

» PREPARE: Open 32 jump rings and close 8 jump rings.

Make the Earrings

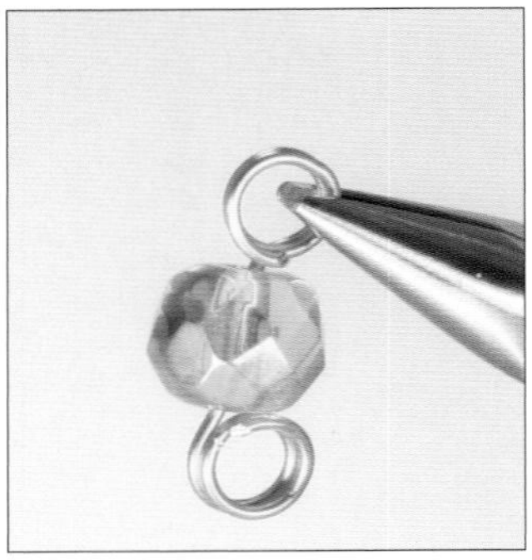

1. Cut two 4" pieces of 18-gauge wire.

2. Make two double-loop bead connectors (see "Making Double-Loop Bead Connectors," p. 16).

3. Take one open jump ring and scoop up two closed jump rings and one end of a connector. Close the jump ring.

4. Take a second open jump ring and scoop up the two closed jump rings added in step 3 and the connector. Close the jump ring.

5. Hold your work by the double ring of the connector added in step 3. Fold down the two closed jump rings added in step 3, one on either side of the two open jump rings added in steps 3 and 4.

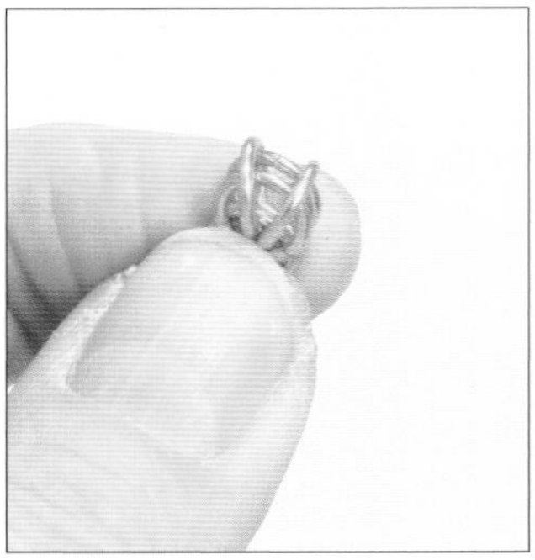

6. Push the two folded down jump rings up using your thumb and forefinger. As you can see, the two open jump rings added in steps 3 and 4 will spread apart, exposing the two closed rings you flipped. Some of my students refer to this as "opening the duck's mouth and revealing his tongue".

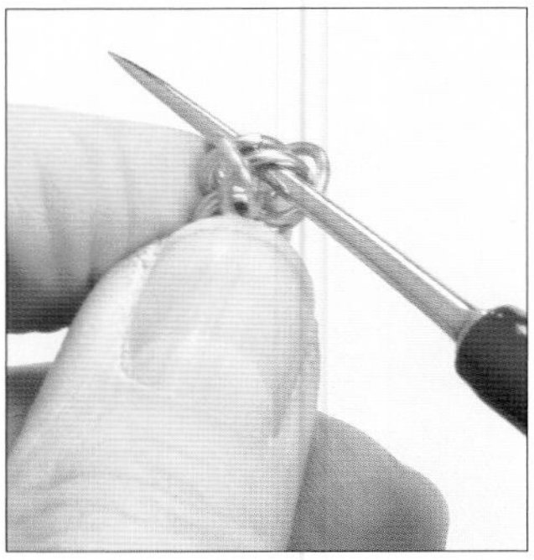

7. I have inserted a beading awl (or you can use a 9" piece of craft wire) showing you where your next three jump rings will go. You can keep the awl there until you get your first jump ring through the proper jump rings.

8. Take one open jump ring and scoop up the two flipped jump rings from inside the duck's mouth. Close the jump ring.

9. Take a second open jump ring and scoop up the same two flipped jump rings as in step 8. Close the jump ring.

10. Take a third open jump ring and repeat step 9. Close the jump ring.

11. Take one open jump ring and scoop up the three jump rings added in steps 8–10. Before closing, add two closed jump rings. Close the jump ring.

12. Take a second open jump ring and scoop up the three open jump rings added in steps 8–10 and the two closed jump rings added in step 11. Close the jump rings.

13. Hold your work by the three open jump rings added in steps 8–10 and fold down the two closed jump rings added in step 11 (as you did in steps 5–7).

14. Take one open jump ring and scoop up the two flipped jump rings from inside the duck's mouth. Close the jump ring.

15. Take a second open jump ring and scoop up the same two flipped jump rings as in step 14. Close the jump ring.

16. Take a third open jump ring and scoop up the same two flipped jump rings as in step 14. Close the jump ring.

17. Working from one side, take one open jump ring and scoop up the jump rings added in step 3 and the jump rings added in step 8. Close the jump ring.

18. Take one open jump ring and scoop up the same two jump rings you picked up in step 17 and also go through the jump ring added in step 17. Close the jump ring. This will make a two-ring möbius.

19. Repeat step 17, this time going through both the jump rings added in step 17 and step 18. Close the jump ring. Now you have a three-ring möbius.

Color Option

20. Working along the opposite side, repeat steps 17–19 using the two jump rings from steps 4 and 9 on the other side.

21. Open the loop of an earring wire and add the other end of the connector. Close the earring wire.

22. Repeat to make a second earring.

🛈 **TIP**

When opening earring wires, open them the same way you would a jump ring: twist toward you. Because these earrings have a closed double loop at the top, I had to open the earring wire instead of adding a jump ring. If I had added a jump ring, the orientation of the earring would be wrong.

Turquoise Beaded Earrings

My birthstone happens to be turquoise, so I wanted to incorporate the color into this book. What better way to do it than with these cute little earrings with beads that look like pearls! Feel free to add beads to every jump ring, as I did in the pink version on p. 109.

» PREPARE: Open all of the jump rings. Add two beads to 8 of the open jump rings, and close those jump rings.

Make the Earrings

materials

» **24** jump rings (turquoise enamel-coated copper)
» **16** 6º seed beads (white Czech glass)
» **1** pair earring wires (see "Making Earring Wires," p. 14)

tools

» **2** pairs chainnose, snubnose, or flatnose pliers

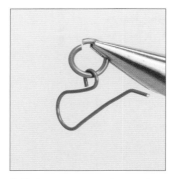

1. Take one open jump ring and scoop up one earring wire. Close the jump ring.

2. Take one open jump ring and scoop up the jump ring added in step 1. Close the jump ring.

3. Take a second jump ring and repeat step 2.

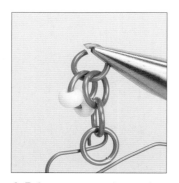

4. Take one open jump ring and scoop up just the jump ring added in step 2. Before closing, add one of the closed beaded jump rings. Close the jump ring.

5. Take one open jump ring and scoop up just the jump ring added in step 3. Before closing, add one of the closed beaded jump rings. Close the jump ring.

6. Take one open jump ring and pick up both of the closed beaded jump rings between the two sets of beads. Close the jump ring.

7. Take a second open jump ring and pick up both of the closed beaded jump rings between the two sets of beads. Before closing the jump ring, go through the jump ring added in step 6. Close the jump ring.

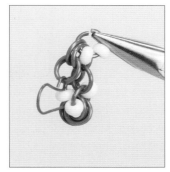

8. Take a third open jump ring and pick up both of the closed beaded jump rings between the two sets of beads. Before closing, go through the jump ring added in steps 7 and 6. Close the jump ring.

9. Open up one of the beaded jump rings just enough to scoop up from the front the two jump rings added in steps 2 and 3. Close the jump ring.

10. Take a second beaded jump ring and repeat step 9, but this time, scoop up the same two jump rings from the back.

11. Repeat to make a second earring.

Design Option

TIP

Not all beads within the same package have the same size hole and will fit the jump rings. If the bead won't fit, put it aside so you won't try to use it again and find another one. The beads may not go past the bottom center of the jump ring until the jump ring is closed.

ACKNOWLEDGMENTS

First I would like to thank my publisher, Kalmbach Books, for allowing me to write this book. The concept was a great one: Use one size jump ring for the whole book! Brilliant! I would also like to thank my editor, Erica Swanson. Without her help and commitment, this book may not have been written.

Thanks to Linda Franzblau for believing in me and assisting me at all of the CHA shows with make & takes. You have been an invaluable help to me.

I would like to thank Beadalon and Parawire for their generous donation of wire and jump rings!

Also, my husband Shan, for putting up with my long hours and my consistent mumbling around the house while making this book! Your support means the world to me.

And lastly, to my two crazy dogs, Miss Gizmo a deer-faced Chihuahua, and Miss Zipper, a multi-poo. They have both been by my side, whether I am at my desk writing, taking pictures, or working from my bed in front of the television.

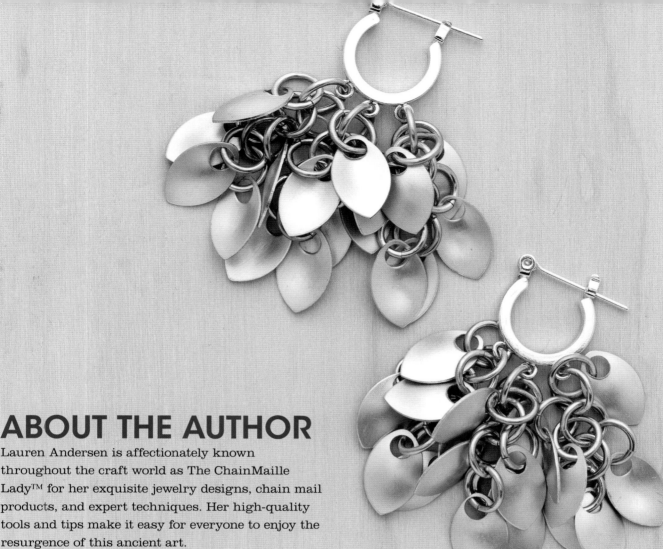

ABOUT THE AUTHOR

Lauren Andersen is affectionately known throughout the craft world as The ChainMaille Lady™ for her exquisite jewelry designs, chain mail products, and expert techniques. Her high-quality tools and tips make it easy for everyone to enjoy the resurgence of this ancient art.

Chain mail was originally used as a type of metal armor around 400 B.C., consisting of small metal rings linked together in a pattern to form a mesh. Today, Lauren weaves chain mail from sterling silver, Artistic Wire®, aluminum, and other metals, at times incorporating crystals or other gems. She has created some of the most intricate and beautiful modern jewelry designs found anywhere.

As an acclaimed chain mail designer, instructor, product developer, author, media contributor, and international spokesperson, Lauren enjoys sharing her passion for the technique, beauty, and symmetry of chain mail.

Lauren has been a frequent guest on television shows including Beads, Baubles & Jewels and the Jewelry Television network's Jewel School. Her designs have been published in the popular industry magazine Step by Step Wire Jewelry, including being featured on the front page.

Lauren is the author of three other leading chain mail books: Basics of Chain Maille, Advanced Chain Maille, and The Absolute Beginners Guide: Making Chain Mail Jewelry. Her unique designs are inspired by geometric shapes, patterns, and angles, as well as innovative techniques.

As an international spokesperson with the Beadalon® Design Team, she travels around the country demonstrating chain mail methods and presenting her product line, including The ChainMaille Lady™ Snub Nose Pliers and The ChainMaille Lady™ Travel Kit.

Lauren lives in the San Gabriel Valley of sunny southern California with her husband and ally Shan, who has earned the title Mr. Chain.

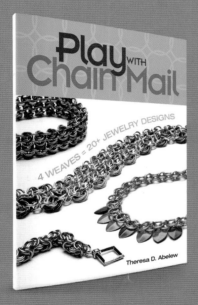

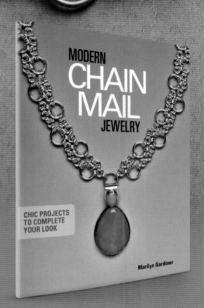